KEY TO

Writing

BOOK 4

CHRISTINE MOORCROFT ◆ LES RAY

Published by Letts Educational
The Chiswick Centre
414 Chiswick High Road
London W4 5TF
Tel: 020 8996 3333
Fax: 020 8742 8390
E-mail: mail@lettsed.co.uk
Website: www.letts-education.com

Letts Educational is part of the Granada Learning Group. Granada Learning is a division of
Granada plc.

First published 2003

ISBN 184085 9075

British Library Cataloguing in Publication Data
A catalogue record for this book is available from the British Library.

Concept development, design and production for Letts Educational by Start to Finish,
 9 Whitecross Square, Cheltenham GL53 7AY

Commissioned by Kate Newport
Project management by Phillipa Allum
Designed and typeset by Paul Manning
Production by PDQ
Printed and bound in Italy by Amilcare Pizzi

Introduction for Teachers or Parents

The activities in this series focus on writing skills and use a
range of models.

The passages have been selected from the range of text-types
advocated by the National Literacy Strategy to give the children
an awareness of all types of writing, from fiction by
acknowledged writers to non-fiction and real-life texts.

The passages are intended for use during shared reading
activities and therefore may be at a higher level than the
reading age of some of the children.

The first activity in each unit encourages the children to
investigate the texts and consider important features and
characteristics of style. Most children should be able to
complete these activities.

The second activity in each unit requires the children to use
the passage as a model and to write in the style of the passage,
using the important features they have identified. The writing
tasks are fairly simple and short because they are related to the
passage and the skills will need to be modelled by the teacher.

The third activity in each unit fosters the development of the
children's own writing. This writing is supported by
photocopiable activity sheets in the Teacher's Book and so
differentiation in ability level is by outcome.

An added feature of this series, from Book 3 onwards, is the
inclusion of suggestions for presentation and use of ICT as an
integral part of the writing process.

Contents

Fire!

In his autobiography, Laurie Lee describes an event from his childhood.

Then the schoolhouse chimney caught fire. A fountain of sparks shot high into the night, writhing and sweeping on the wind, falling and dancing along the road. The chimney hissed like a firework, great rockets of flame came gushing forth, emptying the tiny house, so that I expected to see chairs and tables, knives and forks, radiant and burning, follow. The moss-tiles smouldered with sulphurous soot, yellow jets of smoke belched from cracks in the chimney. We stood in the rain and watched entranced, as if the sight had been saved for this day. As if the house had been saved, together with the year's bad litter, to be sent up in flames and rejoicing.

How everyone bellowed and scuffled and sang, drunk with their beer and the sight of the fire.

USEFUL WORDS

autobiography, belched, bellowed, chimney, dramatic, emptying, entranced, expected, fountain, gushing, hissed, knives, paragraph, radiant, rejoicing, setting, smouldered, sulphurous, writhing

1 How does the writer feel about the fire at the schoolhouse?
2 What time of day does the fire happen?
3 How does this make the scene more dramatic?
4 What is the weather like?

a

1 What words does the author use to describe the fire? Copy and complete the chart.
2 Describe the pictures which these words give you, for example: *A fountain sprays high into the air. This gives me a picture of the sparks shooting upwards like water from a fountain.*
3 Write another paragraph about the fire. Describe what happens next.

What he describes	Words used
sparks	fountain
chimney	

b

Describe a dramatic festival bonfire. Write a letter to a friend in another country to tell him or her about it.

◆ Which festival is it? Does it take place in the day or at night? What is the weather like?
◆ List some words which you could use to show your excitement.

c

◆ Use a computer to plan and write your letter.
◆ Insert some pictures using clip art, or scan in some photographs of bonfires.

MAKE YOUR WORK LOOK GOOD!

2 I'm Scared!

Nick and Carrie have to walk through a scary wood.

'There's nothing *to* mind,' she said to Nick as they trudged along the railway line. 'What is there to be scared of? Just a few old trees.'

Nick said nothing; only sighed.

Carrie said, 'All that queer place stuff is just Auntie Lou being superstitious. You know how superstitious she is, touching wood and not walking under ladders and throwing salt over her shoulder when she's spilled some. I'm not surprised Mr Evans gets cross with her sometimes. She's so scared, she'd jump at her own shadow.'

But when they reached the Grove, Carrie felt a little less bold. It was growing dusk; stars were pricking out in the cold sky above them. And it was so quiet, suddenly, that their ears seemed to be singing.

Carrie whispered, 'There's a path down there. By that stone.'

Nick's pale face glimmered as he looked up at her. He whispered back, 'You go. I'll wait here.'

'Don't be silly.' Carrie swallowed — then pleaded with him. 'Don't you want a nice mince pie? We might get a mince pie. And it's not far. Auntie Lou said it wasn't far down the hill. Not much more than five minutes.'

Nick shook his head. He screwed up his eyes and put his hands over his ears.

USEFUL WORDS

atmosphere, fiction, font, ghosts, glimmered, haunted, information, minutes, railway, reached, scared, scary, shoulder, sighed, superstitious, swallowed, trudged, whispered

1 At what time of day are Nick and Carrie walking through the wood?

2 How does this add to the scary atmosphere?

3 Find words which show they are afraid.

4 How does the way they speak show they are afraid?

1 What do you think makes a place scary?

2 What information are you given in the passage which could make the scene even more scary?

3 What do you think will happen next? Continue the story.

Silence?
Night time?
Shadows?

Imagine you have been dared to go into a house which people think is haunted. Describe the house and how you feel about it.

- What do you know about the house which makes you feel afraid?
- Is it night time or day time?
- Think about sounds. Does the front door creak? Do bats flutter and squeak?

- Plan and word-process your story and insert some pictures.
- Publish your work, using 'scary' fonts and borders.

MAKE YOUR WORK LOOK GOOD!

The Big Friendly Giant

The Big Friendly Giant (BFG) has kidnapped Sophie.

Back in the cave, the Big Friendly Giant sat Sophie down once again on the enormous table. 'Is you quite snugly there in your nightie?' he asked. 'You isn't fridgy cold?'

'I'm fine,' Sophie said.

'I cannot help thinking,' said the BFG, 'about your poor mother and father. By now they must be jipping and skumping all over the house shouting "Hello, hello where is Sophie gone?"'

'I don't have a mother and father,' Sophie said. 'They both died when I was a baby.'

'Oh, you poor little scrumplet!' cried the BFG. 'Is you not missing them very badly?'

'Not really,' Sophie said, 'because I never knew them.'

'You is making me sad,' the BFG said, rubbing his eyes.

'Don't be sad,' Sophie said. 'No one is going to be worrying too much about me. That place you took me from was the village orphanage. We are all orphans in there.'

'You is a norphan?'

USEFUL WORDS

badly, character, describe, died, enormous, father, knew, missing, mother, orphan, playscript, really, rubbing, shouting, village, worrying

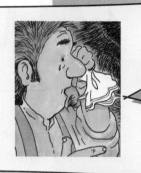

a

1 What sort of character do you expect a giant to be?
2 How is the BFG different from other giants you have read about?
3 What does the BFG's name tell you about the character?

b

1 Collect three examples from the passage to show that the BFG is concerned and kind.
2 Re-write the examples you find to give the opposite impression of the giant, for example: *'I hope you are really cold just sitting there in your nightie.'*
3 Write about what happens next. Write the speech in the same way to make the character likeable.

c

Choose a wicked character from a legend or a fairy tale, for example: the Big Bad Wolf. Write a story in which he or she is a likeable character.

- Think of a situation in which the character could be wicked but turns out to be kind.
- Describe the character.

- Write your story as a playscript. Use a computer. Set it out correctly (see Unit 7).
- Find pictures of fairy-tale characters in books and on the Internet. Display them next to your story.

MAKE YOUR WORK LOOK GOOD!

4 Miss Slighcarp

A mysterious governess arrives to look after Bonnie and Sylvia while their parents are away.

'Don't speak to me in that way, miss!' retorted Miss Slighcarp in a rage. 'You have been spoiled all your life, but we shall soon see who is going to be mistress now. Go to your place and sit down. Do not speak until you are spoken to.'

Bonnie paid not the slightest attention. 'Who said you could wear my mother's best gown?' she repeated. Sylvia, alarmed, had slipped into her place at the table, but Bonnie, reckless with indignation, stood in front of the governess, glaring at her.

'Another word and it's the dark cupboard and bread-and-water for you, miss,' said Miss Slighcarp fiercely.

'I don't care what you say!' Bonnie stamped her foot. 'Take off my mother's dress!'

Miss Slighcarp boxed Bonnie's ears; Bonnie seized Miss Slighcarp's wrists. In the confusion a bottle of ink was knocked off the table, spilling a long blue trail down the gold velvet skirt. Miss Slighcarp uttered an exclamation of fury.

'Insolent, ungovernable child! You shall suffer for this!' With iron strength she thrust Bonnie into a closet containing crayons, globes and exercise books, and turned the key on her.

USEFUL WORDS

attention, character, containing, cupboard, exclamation, exercise, font, governess, indignation, insolent, knocked, merely, mysterious, reckless, retorted, spoiled, strength, ungovernable, wearing, wrists

1 How do you know from the passage that this story is set in the past?
2 What impression does the first sentence give of the governess?
3 How are the two sisters different in character?
4 List the stages leading up to Bonnie being locked in the cupboard.

a

1 List some of Miss Slighcarp's statements. What do they show about her character?
2 List the words used to describe her speech. What impression do they give?
3 What do you think happens to Bonnie? How does she get her revenge? Write the next part of the story.

b

Imagine that your parents or carers have gone away. You are left in the care of a 'nasty old aunt'. Write about what it is like and what happens to you.

- Describe the aunt as a pleasant character at first.
- How does she change?

c

- Plan and write your story using a computer. Use an 'old-fashioned' font.
- Handwrite your piece of writing with pen and ink using 'copperplate' handwriting.

MAKE YOUR WORK LOOK GOOD!

The Old Steam Train

These pages are from a story for very young children. They show how time (chronology) is used in a simple story.

This is Apple Tree Farm.

This is Mrs. Boot. She has two children, called Poppy and Sam, and a dog called Rusty.

"Hurry up," says Mrs. Boot.

"Where are we going today?" asks Poppy. 'To the old station," says Mrs. Boot.

"What's that noise?"

"It's the train. It's coming," says Mrs. Boot. "Look, it's a steam train," says Poppy. "How exciting."

"We're off," says Sam.

The train chugs slowly down the track. "Doesn't the old station look good now?" says Poppy.

USEFUL WORDS

children, chronology, chugs, coming, exciting, farmer, noise, paragraph, simple, slowly, station, today, track

a

1 Why do young children need pictures as well as words in a story?
2 Name each of the characters in this story.
3 In each of the four scenes, where do the characters move **to** and **from**?

Look for words which give a clue.

4 How do we know that the pages of the story are in the right order?

b

1 Re-write each of the captions for the pictures. Include information about the time and location, for example: *It was three o'clock on the platform of the railway station.*
2 Continue the story in four more pictures with captions. Follow the chronological order.
3 Write the same story in paragraphs without pictures. Use the same order. Add details about time, place, characters — and the dog!

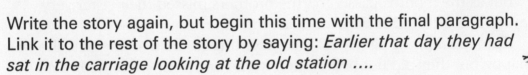

c

Write the story again, but begin this time with the final paragraph. Link it to the rest of the story by saying: *Earlier that day they had sat in the carriage looking at the old station ....*

Which is the more interesting way of writing this story?

◆ Word-process your story. Draw pictures and paste the words under the pictures.
◆ Make books for young children using the stories written by your class.

MAKE YOUR WORK LOOK GOOD!

6 An Indian Folk Tale

Many years ago, there was a large house in a village. Seven brothers and their seven wives lived there all together. The brothers had a young sister who was fifteen and very beautiful. The brothers loved her very much. Their wives kept telling them it was time for her to start her own life, but the brothers ignored them.

A year passed, and when she was sixteen the wives would not be quiet about it any longer. The brothers agreed to arrange a marriage for their sister. They heard of a young, handsome and rich landowner who lived five hundred miles to the south. So they sent their sister's picture and her horoscope to him, the holy man found the best day for the wedding and, at last, the sister was married and left the big house in the village.

But as the months passed by, the brothers missed their sister very much and moaned to their wives all the time.

Eighteen months passed. She kept writing to them saying that she was happy, but they did not believe her. In the end their wives told them to send her an invitation to come and celebrate the New Year festival with them.

USEFUL WORDS

beautiful, believe, brothers, character, festival, folk tale, handsome, horoscope, invitation, italics, marriage, moaned, paragraph, passed, programme, village, wedding, wives

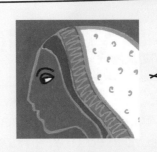

1 What does the first sentence tell us about when the story took place?
2 How old is the sister at the beginning?
3 How old is she at the end of the passage?
4 How much time has passed in the story?

a

Sometimes authors skim over periods of time very quickly, giving just a little information about what happens during that time.

1 Find where this occurs in the story. How much time is missed?
2 Why did the author choose to do this? Why was this time not very important?
3 Write about what happens to the characters in the story during this time.

b

Continue the folk tale. Describe what happens at the festival. Introduce each paragraph with information about how time has passed.

You could do some research on the Hindu New Year festival of Chaitra.

c

♦ Plan and write your folk tale on a computer.
Cut and paste paragraphs so that you can experiment with time order.
♦ Make a book of Indian folk tales for young children.
Write in simple sentences. Illustrate the stories.

MAKE YOUR WORK LOOK GOOD!

When Alice Met Humpty Dumpty

Alice is in the mysterious land through the mirror. She is surprised to see Humpty Dumpty sitting very still on a narrow wall. He does not take any notice of her.

Alice: *(whispering to herself)* He is very like an egg. I would recognise him anywhere.

Humpty Dumpty: *(looking away — very superior)* It is very provoking to be called an egg. Very!

Alice: *(surprised he has heard)* I said you looked like an egg, sir. *(trying to flatter him)* And some are very pretty you know.

Humpty Dumpty: *(still superior, still looking away)* Some people have no more sense than a baby.

Alice: *(not knowing what to do, sings to herself)*

Humpty Dumpty sat on a wall.

Humpty Dumpty had a great fall …

Humpty Dumpty: *(interrupting)* The last line is much too long for the poetry. *(at last he turns to Alice)* Don't stand chattering to yourself like that. Tell me your name and your business.

Alice: My name is Alice, but …

Humpty Dumpty: It's a stupid name. What does it mean?

USEFUL WORDS

actor, bold, business, cast, chattering, flatter, interrupting, italics, mysterious, provoking, recognise, sense, stage directions, superior, surprised, whispering

1 How do you know this is not a story? List the things which make it look different.

2 Explain what the purpose of these features might be in a playscript. Use a chart like this:

Feature of a playscript	Its purpose
Name on left	To tell actors when to speak their parts

a

---

1 Find the words:
   a) with which the author introduces the scene
   b) which help actors to know how to speak their lines
   c) which tell actors how to behave.

2 What kind of character is Humpty Dumpty? Find evidence in the passage. Complete the chart.

What the character is like	Evidence
Thinks he is superior — snooty	He looks away as he speaks to Alice

b

3 Write the next scene in the playscript. Introduce a new character.

Write a playscript using two characters from a well-known fairy tale. Use the correct features of a playscript.

Include stage directions. Describe the scene and the props.

c

◆ Write your script using a computer. Use **bold** for the characters' names and *italics* for the stage directions.

◆ Make a programme for your play. You will need a cast list and some information about the characters.

MAKE YOUR WORK LOOK GOOD!

The Sun and the Wind

This fable was first told around 580BC in Greece by Aesop.

The sun and the wind were having an argument one day about who was the more powerful.

The sun thought he was more powerful because he was all fire and could destroy anything he wanted.

The wind thought he was more powerful because he was all strength and force.

They decided to do one last challenge to decide the case.

A man walked by and they decided to use him as a test. Whoever could make him take off his coat the faster would win.

The wind blew and blew. He tried to tear the coat from the man's back. But the man just hugged the coat to himself even more and struggled on.

The sun decided to be gentle in his approach. He shone down on the man and the man started to become very hot. What did he do? He removed his coat.

The sun had won the battle — not by being fierce and violent, but by being gentle and persistent.

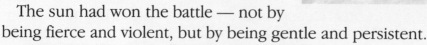

 **USEFUL WORDS**

approach, argument, battle, challenge, destroy, fable, fierce, force, gentle, narrator, persistent, powerful, speech, strength, struggled, thought, violent, whoever

1 How many characters are there in this story? Who are they?
2 What are the main features of these characters?
3 How do you think the characters would speak their lines, for example: boastfully?

a

You are going to plan and write a playscript from the fable.

1 a) Work out a structure for your play. Split the story into scenes.
  b) Think of locations (settings) for the scenes. Add any relevant details.

Scene	Location	Details
1 Sun and wind arguing	In the sky	Clouds blowing by
2 They see man below		

2 Use your plan to write a playscript from the fable. Use all the details and descriptions, the characters and a narrator to tell the story.

b

Find another fable by Aesop, for example: *The Crow and the Cheese* or *The Fox and the Grapes*. Write a playscript based on this fable. Use the correct style.

Do not use speech marks. Put the names of the speakers on the left. Use stage directions.

c

◆ Write your script using a computer (see Unit 7). Find pictures to illustrate it.
◆ Display the fable and the playscript side-by-side in class. Label the features which are the same and those which are different.

MAKE YOUR WORK LOOK GOOD!

The Wind

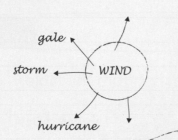

gale
storm
WIND
hurricane

The wind

Nouns

Verbs
raging
calling
wailing

Adjectives

What kind of scene am I imagining?

Kind of scene?
City? Sea? Country?

What time of day is it?

DAY:
clouds
shadows
what I can see
- trees -
branches moving

NIGHT:
shadows
sounds
can't see much

What can make
these noises?
bins flying around
in the street
wires whining
like ghosts

NOISES
whistling
storming
cracking
whooshing
clanging
wailing

What do these remind me of?
Trees, ghosts, storms at sea

What do I
· see?
· feel?
· hear?
· smell?

Wind pushing against me
LIKE
a bad-tempered person
a fire burning

My first draft

It is night time. I struggle against the force of the wind. It is as if I am being punched in the stomach by a bad-tempered person.

The city streets are empty. I can only see the quick shadows of the things being thrown around. A bin lid whizzes past me, clattering and clanging as it goes. It disappears into the darkness. The wires above my head whine and moan as the wind shakes them. It is as if ghosts are flying above my head. They are laughing at me as I fight the force of the wind.

The trees thrash about — their arms bare of leaves. The wind has cruelly stripped them of their clothes and left them to shiver.

The wind is angry. It traps itself behind the buildings and cries out.

USEFUL WORDS

bad-tempered, brainstorming, buildings, clanging, cracking, cruelly, disappearing, draft, ghosts, raging, shadows, stomach, storming, struggle, thrash, wailing, whine, whistling, whooshing

a

1 The first stage of planning is called 'brainstorming'. How many different kinds of brainstorming can you see?
2 What kinds of ideas has this writer thought of?
3 List any facts she uses. Of what do these remind her?
4 Where has the writer set her story?

b

1 Think of the subject again — the wind. Which senses would be affected by it?
2 Make a second draft of the piece of writing. Add detail to improve it.
3 Re-write the scene, changing the setting and the time of day.

Sense	How it would be affected
Sight	
Hearing	
Touch	Wind pushing against me
Taste	
Smell	

c

Write about another kind of weather, for example: rain. Plan your writing using the brainstorming technique.

◆ Choose a setting and a time of day.
◆ How will it affect all your senses?
◆ Think about comparisons to make the scene come alive.
◆ Make a first draft.

◆ Make a large 'brainstorm' for display. What will you need to include?
◆ Word-process your writing. Use the computer to edit your work.

MAKE YOUR WORK LOOK GOOD!

Annie's New Friend

Annie was talking to someone who wasn't there.

Jack looked across the school playground at his sister. She was nodding her head and smiling at the empty space next to her, waving her hands around as she talked. Jack wondered briefly why he was surprised. Nothing Annie did ought to surprise him any more. She was capable of anything, including having a conversation with thin air. Not that he cared what Annie was up to.

'Annie!' he called. 'Go and sit on the wall.'

Annie gave him a big smile.

'Can Sarah come with me?'

'What?' Jack turned to his sister.

'I said, "Can Sarah come with me?"'

'Sarah who?'

'Sarah Slade.' Annie pointed at the empty space next to her, a pleased look on her face.

'This is Sarah. She's my new friend. Say hello to Sarah, Jack.'

'There's no one there,' Jack muttered.

'Yes, there is,' Annie retorted, unruffled. 'She's just invisible, that's all.'

USEFUL WORDS

briefly, capable, conversation, fiction, friend, including, invisible, muttered, nodding, ought, playground, playscript, pointed, retorted, smiling, surprised, talked, unruffled, waving, wondered

1 What are the names of the characters in this story?
2 What do you find surprising about one of the
characters?
3 Do you believe what Annie says about her friend?
4 What does Jack think of Annie? Find evidence.

a

1 What questions do you want to ask after reading the passage?
2 List some interesting features of the characters. How could
these develop in the story? For example: *Annie could be telling
lies. This could get her into trouble.*
3 How could the story or the characters develop? Continue the
story using the information built up so far.

b

Imagine you are followed by a huge,
pink, talking rabbit — but only you
can see it! Write a story about what
happens and how people react to you.

*Think of a
surprise ending —
not just 'And then
I woke up ...'.*

c

♦ Introduce the story with a situation. Invent some characters.
♦ What happens if you talk to the rabbit? What do people think of
you? How do they react to you?

♦ You could present your story as a playscript
(see Unit 7).
♦ Collect your pink rabbit stories in a class anthology,
showing the different endings.
♦ Produce a storyboard for a film of your story.

MAKE YOUR WORK
LOOK GOOD!

The Sandcastle

'I think it's a super castle,' said Biscuits. 'Truly. A fantastic creation. Practically the eighth wonder of the world. Honest Tim.'

'Ooooh! Let's see this super-duper castle, eh?' said a loud voice behind us, making us both jump.

Two boys had crept up behind us. One was about our age and very pale and pinched looking. He didn't look very tough but his smile was spiteful. He was the sort of boy you treated with caution.

The other boy was much bigger. And much tougher too. His hair was shaved so short it was just prickles, which looked as sharp as spikes. If he head-butted you you'd get severely perforated. He was the sort of boy that made a Red Alert system buzz inside your brain.

He was wearing great big Doc Martens even on the beach. I looked at the boy. I looked at the boots. I knew what was going to happen next.

'What a dinky ducky castle you two little cissy boys have made,' he said, his eyes beady. 'Shame it's just sand. Someone could accidentally trip and …'

He kicked hard. The castle collapsed.

USEFUL WORDS   accidentally, beady, castle, caution, character, collapsed, conflict, creation, fantastic, location, perforated, pinched, prickles, setting, spiteful, system, tough, wearing, wonder

1 From which part of the story do you think this passage is taken (the beginning, the middle or the end)? Why do you think that?

2 What is the setting for this story?

3 What are the characters like? Find evidence.

4 Which characters are 'good' and which are 'bad'? Find evidence.

What the character is like	Evidence
Biscuits is friendly and has a sense of humour	Biscuits jokes about the castle

a

1 Why do you think this episode is going to cause the conflict in the story?

2 Write about what you think has happened so far in the build up. Describe the setting and the characters and what they have been doing.

3 Continue the story. What do you think happens as a result of this conflict?

b

Write a story in which a gang force their way into your playground and cause trouble. This is the conflict in your story.

◆ Build up details of setting and character.

◆ Decide what will happen as a result of the conflict.

Will the 'good' characters defeat the 'bad' characters?

c

◆ Plan and write your story using a computer.

◆ Write and print out different endings. Display them to see how they have changed during planning and writing.

MAKE YOUR WORK LOOK GOOD!

Rohan's Secret

Rohan drew so much that the magic pencil was soon worn to a stub. Instead of throwing it away like an ordinary pencil, he took it down to the banyan tree and buried it in the earth at its roots where he had hidden the lump of rubber. As he walked away he worried about whether he would be able to draw as well with an ordinary pencil bought at the stationery shop near the school gate. But he had had so much practice now, and become so good an artist, that he found he could do as good a drawing with the new pencil he bought as with the magic one.

He became so famous in that town that people came from miles away to see the pictures his mother pinned to the walls of their house. They went to school and asked the teacher about him. No one knew how he had learnt to draw and paint so well. Even when he became a great artist, whose name was known all over the land, Rohan did not tell anyone his secret. That was his secret — and the banyan tree's, and they kept it to themselves as secrets should be kept.

USEFUL WORDS

anthology, artist, buried, earth, famous, illustrate, instead, magic, ordinary, pictures, pinned, practice, resolution, secret, stationery, themselves, worn, worried

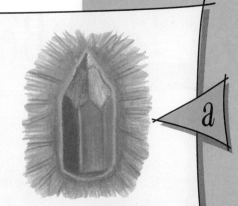

1 What clues are there to suggest that this passage comes from the end of the story?

2 What do you think was 'magic' about the pencil?

3 Explain why Rohan did not need the pencil any longer to be a good artist.

4 Why was Rohan's secret also the banyan tree's secret?

a

1 Write about how Rohan found the magic pencil and what it did to change his life. Think about the details you will use.

2 This story has a happy resolution. Write a sad resolution to the story.

Build-up	Climax	Resolution
Sad child — finds the magic pencil		

b

Write a story in which you become really good at something after finding a magic object.

◆ What is the object? What does it help you to become good at?

◆ What do you do with it in the end?

c

◆ Write your story using a computer.

◆ Print and collect the stories in a class anthology. Discuss the different resolutions.

◆ Write a newspaper article about your amazing skills. Find photographs to illustrate the article.

MAKE YOUR WORK LOOK GOOD!

Bedivere's Betrayal

King Arthur lay dying. He had lost the great battle and many of his knights were dead. Only brave Sir Lucan and Sir Bedivere were left with him.

'Alas,' he said. 'This is a sorry sight. Our plight is a sad one but there is one final duty you, Sir Bedivere, must perform for me.'

'Anything my King,' said the knight. 'I am here to serve you.'

'My time is short. Go forth with my sword Excalibur, which I pulled from the stone when I was but a boy. It must be returned to the Lady of the Lake. Walk yonder a mile from here and you will find a large lake. Throw the sword into the water. Return and tell me what you see.' Excalibur was the most powerful sword in the world, with magical powers.

Bedivere found the lake as the King had said and just as he was about to throw the sword into the dark waters, he heard a voice in his ear.

'Why throw this power away? It could be all yours. You could be the most powerful man in the world with that sword.'

Evil thoughts took over Sir Bedivere's mind. He betrayed his King and broke all his vows as a Knight of the Round Table. He hid the sword in a bush and returned to the King.

USEFUL WORDS battle, betrayed, character, evil, hilt, historical, knights, location, magnificent, obeyed, plight, precious, setting, sword, thought, traitor

1 What do you learn about the location of the story?

2 Who are the characters?
What impression do you get of them?

3 Which words in the passage seem to be old-fashioned?

Use a dictionary to find out what the words mean.

a

---

1 List details from the passage which tell you this is not a modern story.

2 Continue the story. Keep your details correct to the period in history.

Look at what the characters say.

b

Choose a period you are studying in history. Write a story about someone who travels from that time to your school. What would he or she think is strange about life in the twenty-first century?

c

♦ Use the Internet and books to research the history for your story. Find pictures to illustrate it.

♦ Make a set of story cards. Illustrate settings (such as a castle, a cottage), characters (such as barons, kings, peasants) and objects (such as swords). Use them to tell historical stories.

MAKE YOUR WORK LOOK GOOD!

14 Smith and the Blind Man

Smith is a boy pickpocket who lives on the streets in the early nineteenth century. He has been drinking gin.

'Help me up! Help me, I say! For pity's sake, sir! Can't you see I'm blind?'

'A blind man!' gasped Smith. 'Oh Gawd! A mole-in-the-hole!'

The gin's tempest dropped abruptly away and left a glum wreckage behind, bleak and forlorn in the freezing night.

A boy — a child — thought the blind man, uneasily. Most likely a young thief. Most likely he'll rob me and run off — frightened out of his miserable wits. Oh God! How am I to get home?

'If you let go me ankle,' muttered Smith, 'I'll help you up; that's if you're really blind. Can you see me?'

The gentleman shook his head.

'What am I doing now?' asked Smith, pulling a hideous face.

'I don't know — I don't know! I swear I'm blind! Look at my eyes! Any light in 'em? Look at my smoked spectacles. They're somewhere about. Look for …'

'What am I doing now?' demanded Smith pulling another more monstrous face; for he'd help no one who didn't need it.

USEFUL WORDS

abruptly, ankle, character, demanded, forlorn, freezing, frightened, gasped, hideous, historical, likely, miserable, monstrous, muttered, pity, spectacles, tempest, thief, uneasily, wreckage

30

1 What do you think life was like for a child who had to live on the streets at this time?

2 Smith is a pickpocket. Does that make you like him less?

3 Which words in the passage seem to be old-fashioned?

Use a dictionary to find out what the words mean.

a

1 What do you learn about the two characters in the passage?

2 The setting for the story is a street in Victorian London. Think of details to make it as real as possible. Use the chart to help.

Smell	Sight	Hearing	Touch	Taste

3 What does Smith do? Does he rob the man? Does he help him? Use your ideas to continue the story.

b

Imagine you travel back in time to the Victorian period of history. Write about how you meet Smith and become involved in his adventures.

Do some research. What was life like then for people of your age? Was there school? Did you have to work?

c

♦ Use a computer to write a series of different 'What would I have done?' endings for the story. Print and display them. Discuss the different endings.

♦ Produce a fact file about the lives of poor children in Victorian times. Find out about children working in factories and mines. See also Unit 15.

MAKE YOUR WORK LOOK GOOD!

Life in a Workhouse School

A For children who could not afford to pay for their education in the nineteenth century, the workhouse school was the only resort. They got up and made their beds by 6.20 a.m. They had breakfast by 7 a.m. Breakfast consisted of a pint of porridge made with

milk and thickened with flour and a small piece of bread. After breakfast they were allowed to play until 8.45 a.m. when they assembled for prayers and school. Lunch (meat and vegetables or soup thickened with flour) was at 12 noon and school was from 2 p.m. until 5 p.m. The children were again allowed to play until 6 p.m. when they had supper. At 7.45 p.m. they washed, said their prayers and went to bed.

B Let us just think of those poor children who were forced to suffer the terrors of the workhouse school. They would be dragged from sleep at the unearthly hour of 6.20 and then scrubbed and forced to eat gruel — hardly enough to satisfy anyone. These children would have hardly any time to play; instead, day after boring day, they would be forced to sit at their tiny desks for hours and beaten if they did not do as they were told. Such a cruel existence is unbelievable.

USEFUL WORDS

afford, breakfast, children, consisted, cruel, education, existence, fact, nineteenth, non-fiction, opinion, satisfy, scrubbed, terrors, unearthly, until, vegetables

1 Write three facts about your school.
2 Write three opinions about your school.
3 Which passage is fact and which is the opinion of the writer? How do you know?

a

1 Compare the two passages. Find two examples of facts and two examples of opinions in each one.

Passage	Fact	Opinion
A		
B		

2 What sort of writer would only use fact? What sort of writer would use opinion?
3 Continue writing each passage.
   a) In A, give more facts about the life of the children.
   b) In B, write about how you feel about their lives.

b

1 Write a passage about a day at your school as if you were producing a history book.
2 Write a diary entry about a day at your school which gives your opinions.

Write things which can be proved.

How do you feel about what you do?

c

◆ Word-process your writing.
◆ Handwrite a diary of a child in the workhouse. Use the information in the passages.

MAKE YOUR WORK LOOK GOOD!

A Leisure Survey

A recent survey in a large new town reveals many interesting facts concerning how people spend their weekends.

On a typical Saturday morning 37 per cent of the women questioned in the survey go shopping and so do 14 per cent of the men. The latter figure is a high one, as the survey also shows that a third of the men interviewed still work on Saturday mornings.

Shopping is also one of the main occupations of Saturday afternoon. Nearly half of the women go shopping and one in five of the men. Nevertheless, one in ten of the men in the town watch TV in the afternoon and a similar proportion work at their hobbies or play or watch games.

On Saturday evening no less than 60 per cent of the women watch TV. Of the remainder, 10 per cent say that they entertain friends; 10 per cent go to the cinema; and five men out of every hundred go to a bar or public house.

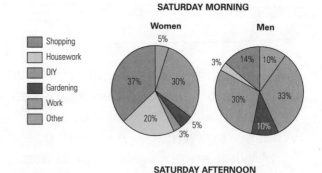

SATURDAY MORNING

Shopping
Housework
DIY
Gardening
Work
Other

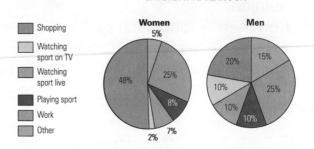

SATURDAY AFTERNOON

Shopping
Watching sport on TV
Watching sport live
Playing sport
Work
Other

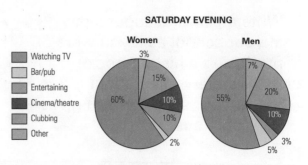

SATURDAY EVENING

Watching TV
Bar/pub
Entertaining
Cinema/theatre
Clubbing
Other

a

1 What is the purpose of this piece of writing?
2 Where would you find such a piece of writing?
3 Does it contain facts or the views of the writer
   — or both?
4 Reports help to organise and record
   information. In which other subjects at school
   do you write reports?

b

1 What does the first paragraph of this report
   aim to do?
   What does the rest of the report contain?
2 What is the subject of each of the four paragraphs?
3 Which tense is used in this report?
4 Write the next paragraph of the report, about
   what people do on Sunday.

Make up some information to help.

c

Carry out a survey of your classmates to find out which TV
programmes they watch and how long they spend watching
them. Write a report to be shared with younger children.

Produce charts and graphs to illustrate your report.

♦ Use a computer to draw the charts and graphs.
♦ Write and print questionnaires for other surveys.
♦ Design and print a large poster explaining the features
   of a report. Display it with examples from your report.

MAKE YOUR WORK
LOOK GOOD!

Silly News Weekly

HORROR AS MARY'S PEN PLUNGES FROM DESK

Yesterday at an inner-city primary school, there was confusion and shock when a pen plunged from a desk and hit the floor.

The pen, a new blue cartridge pen especially purchased for school by her 80-year-old grandmother, belonged to golden-haired Mary Smith — a Year 4 pupil at Stonard Primary School in London's Docklands area — and is now totally useless.

Could do nothing about it

When interviewed Mary said, 'It happened at about ten to two. I was just starting to think about my English work so I looked for my new pen. It had completely disappeared.' She was too upset to speak for a moment. The shocked and shaken Mary continued, 'Suddenly I saw it, which was a relief because I thought my friends were playing a joke. But then it started to roll away and I could do nothing about it.'

Tracy blames the boys

Her friend Tracy — a lively, dark-haired sporty-type, also in Year 4 — told us in confidence that she thought the boy at the next table must have deliberately wobbled the desk so the new pen fell. 'Just the kind of thing a boy would do,' she sneered scornfully.

Mary's teacher, Mr Barton (32 and slightly balding), said that he was looking into the matter and held up the pen with bent nib for us to see. The class were still in a state of shock about such a terrible event, and the school has issued a warning to the general public to look out for young pen vandals and to keep all writing equipment safe.

USEFUL WORDS

confusion, continued, deliberately, disappeared, equipment, especially, grandmother, headline, inform, interviewed, lively, newspaper article, plunged, relief, sneered, terrible, useless

a

1 What is the purpose of this piece of writing?
2 How do you know that this is not a serious newspaper article?
3 Does it contain facts or the views of the writer — or both?
4 Newspaper articles inform readers about events, but they need to tempt you to buy the paper. Which features of this article make you want to read on?

b

1 What is the purpose of a headline?
2 What does the first paragraph of this article aim to do? What does the rest of it contain?
3 What is the subject of each of the four paragraphs?
4 Write a paragraph for the article about what other people in the class might have said. Make up some information.

c

Write other silly newspaper articles about unimportant things which happen in your class.

Ask the questions: Who? What? When? Where? How? Why?

Dog Eats Homework

Football lost during break

◆ Write and edit your newspaper article using a computer. Try to make it look as if it is from a real newspaper.
◆ Find photographs on the Internet (or elsewhere). Scan or paste them into your article to make it look more real.

MAKE YOUR WORK LOOK GOOD!

Quick Truffles

These are very light and easy to make, and you can store them in the fridge for up to two weeks. They are excellent coated in chocolate.

You will need:

    125 g of plain chocolate
    125 g of butter
    125 g of icing sugar
    2 teaspoons of instant coffee powder

For the coating:
    2 tablespoons of cocoa powder *or*
    125 g of plain chocolate
    1 teaspoon of olive oil

This is how you make them:

Melt the chocolate and leave to cool.
Beat the butter with the icing sugar until
    light and fluffy.
Mix in the chocolate and the coffee.
Put the mixture in the refrigerator for at
    least an hour until it hardens enough to
    be rolled into balls or sausage shapes.
Roll these in cocoa, or melt the chocolate with the oil and coat each
    truffle in chocolate.
Leave on kitchen foil to set.

USEFUL WORDS

chocolate, coated, cocoa, coffee, easy, excellent, flow chart, fluffy,
icing, instructions, kitchen, layout, refrigerator, sausage, truffle

1 Why do people write instructions in this way?

2 What would happen if you tried to make Quick Truffles without instructions?

3 What do you notice about the layout of these instructions? How is this helpful?

a

1 Copy and complete the flow chart.

2 Write out and number the six steps needed to make truffles.

3 Change the order of the six steps. What is the effect of this?

4 Write simple instructions for a visiting alien on how to make a cup of tea.

Features of instructions

1 Title

▼

2 A list of what you will need

▼

3

▼

b

Make up a name for a game and write instructions.

◆ Describe the aim of the game.

◆ Tell people what they will need.

◆ Explain what to do at each stage.

◆ Use verbs which tell people to do things, for example: *Throw the dice*.

c

◆ Word-process and print out your work.

◆ Design and make a box for your game.

◆ Draw an interesting picture for the lid of the box.

MAKE YOUR WORK LOOK GOOD!

A Trip to the Zoo

How to get to ...

LETTSTOWN ZOO

If you want to see the snakes ...

Go in the main entrance from Marsh Street. Then turn right at the first crossroads into Right Avenue. The pond is on your left. Now, carry on along Right Avenue. The road curves around. You will pass the penguins on your left. Finally, take the next turning to the left called Fish Road. The snakes are on your right.

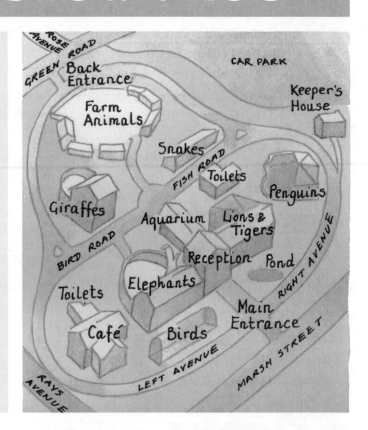

USEFUL WORDS

aquarium, avenue, command, crossroads, directions, elephants, entrance, exit, first, giraffes, instructions, label, left, penguins, reception, right, road, second, straight, street, tense, turn

1 How is this piece of writing trying to help the reader? What is its aim?

2 Where else at school or at home might you find similar pieces of writing?

3 How does the map make the instructions easier to understand?

Place	Type of instruction
Home	How to find a restaurant

a

1 List words which are useful in giving people directions.

2 Write the verbs used in the passage. What tense is used? What else do the verbs have in common?

3 List any words at the beginning of sentences which help to link together a series of steps.

4 Write instructions to help someone to get from the giraffes to the penguins.

b

Imagine your school has become a very famous building because some treasure has been found under the playground. Write instructions to help people to find it from a nearby place.

Write your instructions in the correct order. Use direction words. Use the command form of verbs.

c

◆ Write your instructions on a computer.

◆ Find free street maps of your local area on the Internet to help make the instructions clear.

◆ Draw a plan of your school and label all the rooms and include it with your instructions.

MAKE YOUR WORK LOOK GOOD!

How to Fly a Hot Air Balloon

A hot air balloon consists of a basket, four big gas tanks, a burner and the balloon or 'envelope'.

First, the pilot puts four nylon poles into sockets on top of the basket. Then she puts the burner on top of the poles. Next, she connects the cables to the burner frame. The cables also go under the basket to hold everything together.

After this, she connects the hoses from the full gas tanks to the burner and tests it.

Next, two people hold the mouth of the balloon open while it is filled with cold air from the fan until it is quite fat and tight.

Now for the difficult bit. The pilot lies on the ground, half in the basket. She turns on the gas burner and points the flame into the 'mouth' of the balloon. Slowly the balloon stands up.

When the pilot is ready to go, she heats up the air in the balloon a bit more. When the air is hot enough the balloon will rise off the ground.

USEFUL WORDS

balloon, basket, burner, cables, connects, diagram, difficult, explanation, label, mouth, nylon, paragraph, properly, sockets, technical

1 What is the purpose of an explanation?
2 Where else at school or at home might you find explanations?
3 What does the first paragraph of this explanation aim to do?
4 What does the rest of the passage contain?

1 What is the subject of each paragraph?
2 Write down the verbs used in the passage. What tense is used?
3 List words which would be useful for explaining things.
4 Is the information written in any particular order? Why is this important when explaining?
5 Make notes from the explanation. Write a list of numbered points explaining the steps to make a hot air balloon fly.
6 Write another paragraph explaining what passengers would have to do when they are in the air.

Choose a difficult topic from another subject, for example: the water cycle. Write an explanation of the process.

Diagrams will help.

◆ Draw diagrams and label them. Add notes to explain parts of the diagrams. Put the notes in boxes.
◆ List the technical words you use in a glossary, giving their meanings.

MAKE YOUR WORK LOOK GOOD!

The Wild West

Pushing West

By the 1850s thousands of people had journeyed for months along treacherous trails. They crossed fast-flowing rivers and rocky mountains in their search for land to farm.

Skull of a longhorn cow

Pioneer trails were often marked with broken wheels, discarded furniture, and animal skulls. The longhorn cow was the commonest cow in America until the 1880s.

Some pioneers were looking for land

Covers were made from canvas and waterproofed with paint or linseed oil

Two horses are pulling this wagon. Most of the pioneer wagons were pulled by oxen or mules.

The search for land
Pioneer families carried all their belongings in covered wagons. The journey was long and hard — pioneers faced cold weather, illness, bad food, and harsh terrain.

Others were lured by news of a gold rush

Go for gold!
In 1849 over 80,000 people flooded west, hoping to make their fortunes. Few did, but they created instant, and often lawless, towns.

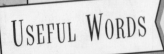

USEFUL WORDS

America, belongings, bullet point, caption, crossed, fact, families, font, fortune, furniture, hoping, instant, journey, lawless, mountains, pioneer, subheading, thousands, trail, treacherous, waterproofed

a

1 What information do the pictures give?
2 There is a caption for each picture. What is their purpose?
3 Does the writer give you fact or opinion?
4 Designers help authors to make information easy to understand. What features do this in the passage?

b

1 Which words do you first notice when you look at the pages? Why?
2 How many different sizes and kinds of fonts can you find? Make a list and say what each one is used for.
3 Write out each paragraph using subheadings. Write them out again giving each fact a separate bullet point. What difference do bullet points make?
4 Write a paragraph describing the covered wagon in the picture.

c

Do some research into Native Americans. Write a page about one aspect of their life for an information book about them.

Do not put too much on the page. The information needs to be clear.

Use organisational devices: subheadings, bullets, bold text, pictures, captions, fact boxes, etc.

♦ Use the Internet and books for your research, and to find pictures to illustrate your writing.
♦ Write and edit your page using a computer.
♦ Collect your pages together. Publish them as a book on Native Americans and their way of life.

MAKE YOUR WORK LOOK GOOD!

22 London

London is the capital city of the United Kingdom. It covers approximately 1600 km² and has a population of more than 9 million people.

The city was founded by the Romans as Londinium in AD43. It was situated on a terrace near the north bank of the river Thames. The Thames is tidal, and London has been a convenient port since this time.

London is the largest city in the UK and this reflects its importance as Europe's leading financial centre (banking and insurance). Industry has declined over the years and has moved from the centre to the suburbs.

London has mild winters (an average of 6° C in January). Summers are not usually very hot, with an average of 18° C. The average rainfall is 600 mm. Rainfall is heaviest in the autumn months.

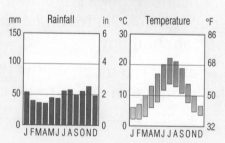

USEFUL WORDS

approximately, average, capital city, centre, convenient, diagram, fact, founded, heaviest, importance, industry, million, non-chronological, opinion, organise, population, rainfall, report, situated, suburbs

a

1 What is the purpose of this piece of writing? Where would you find it?
2 Is it fiction or non-fiction? Does it contain facts or opinions — or both?
3 This report does not follow a time sequence (*first*, *second* … *then*). How is it organised?
4 Reports help to organise and record information. In which subjects at school do you write reports like this one?

A non-chronological report does not follow a time sequence

b

1 What is the subject of each of the four paragraphs?
2 How do maps and diagrams help in a report?
3 Which verb tense is used in this report? Find examples.
4 Think of another topic about London, for example: why do tourists visit? Write another paragraph for the report. Find some information to help.

c

Write a non-chronological report for a geography book about a country you have studied.

List the topic headings you will write about, for example: Location, Size, Population.

◆ Plan and write your report on a computer. Search the Internet for free maps and diagrams.
◆ Combine your reports to make a geography book.

MAKE YOUR WORK LOOK GOOD!

Children's Games

Onward go the blind.
Very slowly as they walk.
All is a shadow.

Clip, clop, boys on stilts.
Snicker-snacker, here they come —
Towering giants!

Riding a barrel
Galloping down rolling streets
But getting nowhere.

There are boys banging,
Scuffling and hitting wood now.
Hitting sticks on bricks.

Hop on the child's train.
It won't take you very far —
Running in a line.

USEFUL WORDS anthology, haiku, hitting, nowhere, onward, rhyme, rhythm, riding, rolling, running, scuffling, shadow, syllable, towering, train

This kind of poem is called a haiku.

1 Each haiku opposite is about a game in the painting. Find each one.
2 How many lines does each poem have?
3 Do they rhyme? What pattern do they follow?
4 Count the number of syllables in each line.

a

1 Choose some other games in the picture. Describe what you think is happening.
2 Write a haiku about one of the games. Use the pattern in the chart.
3 Revise your haiku so that it follows the pattern. Check that it has the correct number of syllables in each line.

Line 1	What you see in the picture
Line 2	Describe it in a different way
Line 3	A surprise ending. Comment on what you see.

b

Look at copies of paintings. Find one you like. Write three haiku about the picture to tell the story.

Follow the pattern for writing a haiku.

c

◆ Write your haiku using a brush or a pen and ink.
◆ Write on textured paper.
◆ Illustrate your haiku with details copied from the painting.

MAKE YOUR WORK LOOK GOOD!

A fly and a flea in a flue
Were imprisoned, so what could they do?
Said the fly, 'Let us flee!'
'Let us fly!' said the flea,
So they flew through a flaw in the flue.

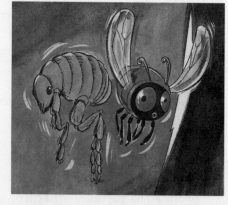

There was a young man from Peru
Who believed that a secret he knew.
That secret was flight,
So he sailed like a kite,
If only this story were true!

A thrifty young fellow of Shoreham
Made brown paper trousers and wore 'em.
He looked nice and neat
Till he bent in the street
To pick up a pin; then he tore 'em.

USEFUL WORDS

anthology, believed, flew, flue, imprisoned, knew, limerick, pattern, rhyme, rhythm, sailed, secret, syllable, thrifty, trousers

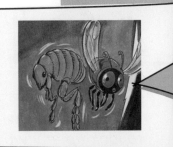

a

1. How many lines does each limerick have?
2. Do they rhyme? What pattern do they follow?
3. Count the syllables in each line.
4. What do you notice about the syllables in the first line?

b

1. What do you notice about the story told by a limerick? Complete a chart.
2. Write your own limerick. Follow the same pattern, for example: *There was a young girl from Dundee.*
   - Think of rhymes for the first line (these will help you with lines 2 and 5).
   - You could end with *That was the young girl from Dundee* to help.

Line 1	A person and a place	Rhymes with line 2
Line 2	Says more about line 1	
Line 3	Shorter — makes a joke	

c

Think of some cartoon characters. Write limericks about the things which happen to them, for example: *There was a young mouse called Mickey ....*

Follow the pattern for writing a limerick.

Don't forget the joke!

- Make up a catchy title for your limerick.
- Draw a cartoon-style illustration for it.
- Copy it in your best handwriting.
- Display the title, the illustration and your limerick on a coloured background.

MAKE YOUR WORK LOOK GOOD!

The Poplar Field

This poem was written in the eighteenth century. Use a dictionary to look up any words you do not understand.

The poplars are fell'd, farewell to the shade
And the whispering sound of the cool colonnade;
The winds no longer sing in the leaves,
Nor the river on this surface their image receives.

Twelve years have elapsed since I first took a view   5
Of my favourite field, and the bank where they grew;
And now in the grass, there they are laid,
And the tree is my seat that once gave me shade.

The blackbird has fled to another retreat
Where the hazels afford him a screen from the heat;   10
And the scene where his music so charmed me before
Resounds with his sweet-flowing music no more.

My fugitive years are all hasting away,
And I will before long lie as lowly as they,
With a turf on my breast and a stone at my head,   15
Before another such grove shall rise in its stead.

by William Cowper

USEFUL WORDS

another, elapsed, farewell, favourite, field, fugitive, future, grove,
image, leaves, past, present, resounds, retreat, rise, scene, screen,
tense, verb, whispering

a

1 What has happened to the poplar trees?
2 How long ago is it since the poet first saw the trees?
3 Where are they now? How does the author feel about this?

b

1 Show what the poet says happens in the past, the present and the future.

Happened in the past	Happening now	Will happen
	He is in a field	

2 For the present, the past and the future, list the verbs used.
3 Re-write the verses using different tenses, for example: verse 1 in the past tense (*The poplars were fell'd ...*); verse 2 in the future tense (*Twelve years will elapse ...*).

c

Write your own life story (autobiography) using the correct verb tenses: *Today I am ..., Last year I was ..., In five years time I shall be ....*

Include a family tree and pictures.

◆ Draw a time-line for your life. Find photographs to illustrate it.
◆ Add a section for the future. Draw what you would like to be like then.

MAKE YOUR WORK LOOK GOOD!

High

Fly, kite!
High!
Till you touch the sky!
Stoop, whistling in the wind;
And whisper down the quivering string.   5
If, as you soar, you find
The world we tread is like a ball —
With mounds for hills, and ponds for seas,
Its oxen small as creeping bees,
Mere bushes its huge trees!   10
But ah, the dew begins to fall,
The evening star to shine,
Down you must sink to earth again —
An earth, I mean, like mine.

by Walter de la Mare

USEFUL WORDS

action verb, begins, creeping, earth, evening, high, mounds, quivering, soar, stoop, synonym, thesaurus, touch, tread, whisper, whistling

a

1 List the verbs the poet uses. Say which tense is used.
2 What kinds of actions does the poet describe?
3 Explain what the poet sees as he looks up at the kite.
4 What does he imagine the world to look like from the kite's point of view?

b

1 Find other verbs (synonyms) for those in the poem. Use a thesaurus.

Verb in the poem	Other verbs (synonyms)
fly	soar, zoom

2 Which of the verbs you found are not suitable to describe the actions of the kite? Why?
3 What do verbs such as *whistling* and *whisper* also describe, beside actions?
4 Describe what it feels like flying a kite on a windy day. Use the action verbs you have collected.

c

Write a poem about a bird flying high into the air. Use action verbs. It does not have to rhyme.

Follow the pattern of 'High'. Use a thesaurus.

◆ Write your poem on the shape of a flying bird. Display it on a blue (sky) background.
◆ Make lists of action verbs. Use a thesaurus. Display the verbs on labels attached to the string of a kite or hanging from a bird mobile.

MAKE YOUR WORK LOOK GOOD!

The History of Ice-Skating

The Vikings probably invented ice-skating. They made skates from polished bones tied to their feet with strips of leather. In the Middle Ages, skates with metal blades became popular in Holland.

Metal-bladed skates spread to Britain; this is recorded by diary writers such as Samuel Pepys, who mentions skating on the frozen River Thames during the Great Frost of 1683. The world's first ice-skating club was formed in Scotland in 1742 and, later that century, historians tell us that ice-skating was the most popular winter pastime at the French court.

E.W. Bushnell, an American, invented the first all-iron skate in 1850. This had no straps; it was clipped onto a boot. Because of this invention, the first ice-rinks soon appeared in America, Canada and Switzerland.

Nowadays, most ice-skating is of three types: speed skating, figure skating and ice dancing. New technologies have made many improvements to modern skates.

USEFUL WORDS

appeared, century, dancing, diary, different, frozen, historians, invented, invention, leather, movements, needed, pastime, polished, popular, recorded, skating, Thames, topic sentence

1 Why do you think writing is split into paragraphs? What would happen if it were not?
2 Look at the dates in the passage. Do you notice any special order?
3 Explain what each paragraph is about.

1 Each paragraph should have a topic sentence: one which tells you what it is about. Write the topic sentence from each paragraph in the passage. Explain why you have chosen it.
2 For each paragraph, list the facts the writer uses to back up each topic sentence.

Paragraph	Topic sentence	Facts used to back it up

3 Do some research to help you to write a final paragraph about ice-skating today. Where do people skate? When? Why?

Choose a popular sporting activity such as football or skateboarding. Write a short history of it. Use the passage as a model.

Write four or five simple paragraphs.

◆ Draw pictures of sports equipment and of people taking part in the sport.
◆ Write captions for the pictures.
◆ Draw a time-line to show the dates of important developments.

MAKE YOUR WORK LOOK GOOD!

Life in the Second World War

SAVE AND MEND

Daily life in Britain was subject to government restrictions. These were designed to share out all resources and avoid waste. People were encouraged to 'dig for victory' and many had allotments where they grew vegetables.

Covered in swastikas (the emblem of Nazi Germany), Squander Bug was a cartoon character used to persuade Britons not to waste anything.

Women in the Land Army helped to keep Britain supplied with vegetables

The sweets ration in Britain was increased from 50g to 75g a week in 1942. Liquid paraffin was used as an ingredient in cakes. Milk powder and dried eggs were introduced in 1943. Some foods like fish and bananas were rarely seen.

Farmers worked day and night to grow more food. Many women joined the Land Army. In June 1941 clothes rationing began and old clothes had to be recycled. By November 1941 a points rationing system had been introduced that gave everyone 16 points a month, as well as the ordinary rations. These points could be used on anything, even canned food like the American 'Spam'. Soon raw materials were in short supply and recycling paper, glass, and aluminium became vital.

By June 1940 vegetables were even growing in the Tower of London moat! Canned fruit and vegetables appeared in the shops.

USEFUL WORDS

allotments, avoid, daily, designed, encouraged, government, information, joined, non-fiction, ordinary, rationing, recycled, resources, restrictions, share, spider diagram, time-line, vegetables, vital

a

1 From what kind of book does this passage come?
2 Is it fiction or non-fiction? How can you tell?
3 What features are used to make the information easier to understand? (See Unit 21.)

b

1 Look at the pictures. Make notes about what you see. Write a numbered list. Give it a title.
2 Draw a spider diagram showing what the 'government restrictions' were.
3 Draw a time-line for 1940–2, showing what the passage says happened between these dates.
4 Make notes of what the passage says about rationing. Use a chart. Think about what the advantages would be.

Government restrictions

Types of rationing	Advantages
Clothes rationing	No shortage of cloth

c

Design a poster to encourage people in the war to 'Dig for Victory'. Make notes from the passage.

Use questions such as: When? Why? Who?

◆ Carry out a survey of what people in your class eat. Draw charts and graphs to compare this with people's diets in the Second World War.
◆ Make a display about the ways in which you can make notes, for example: using lists, charts, spider diagrams and time-lines.

MAKE YOUR WORK LOOK GOOD!

Stonard Road Primary School have been told that their local playing field is to be used to build new houses. The children wrote to the builders to complain.

A

The Manager
Acme Builders
Kynaston Road
Freetown

Stonard Road
Primary School
Freetown

2 June 20--

Dear Sir

I am writing to tell you that my whole class (4B) is upset because you want to build houses on our playing field.

We all enjoy PE and this playing field is the only place we have to do this.

Our teacher says that it is the law to teach PE, but we will have nowhere for these activities. We will have to hire a coach to go to a playing field miles away. This will be very expensive. We will also have to share this field with two other schools so we will not have as much time.

I hope you will understand our point of view and reconsider your plans.

Yours faithfully
Tracy

B

Acme Builders Kynaston Road Freetown

6 June 20--

Class 4B
Stonard Road Primary School
Freetown

Dear Tracy and Class 4B

Thank you for taking the time to write to tell me how you feel about our new development.

I can understand your disappointment at having to go further to play games but let me explain a few issues to you.

This housing is for people who cannot afford the expensive houses in your area, so it will be of benefit to many young people. As a part of this new development we shall be building a youth club for children in the area.

I see your point of view, but you need to understand that the needs of others are also important.

Please write back if you feel I have not answered your concerns.

Yours sincerely
Bob Builder
Managing Director

USEFUL WORDS

activities, address, argument, build, complain, concerns, development, disappointment, expensive, explain, important, issues, letterhead, nowhere, problems, signature, understand

1 Who wrote the letters? To whom was each letter written?

2 Are the letters formal or personal?

3 What is the purpose of Letter A? Why did Tracy feel the need to write?

4 What is the purpose of Letter B? Why did Bob Builder reply?

a

1 Read the beginnings and endings of the letters. How are they different? What is the reason for this?

	Letter A	Letter B
Beginning	Dear Sir	
Ending		

2 List the arguments Tracy uses to back up her point.

3 List the arguments Bob Builder gives in reply. Which arguments do you think are the best?

4 Write Tracy's reply to Bob, in which she gives more of her views.

b

Imagine your school is to be joined with another school five miles away. You will have to move. Write a letter to your local council explaining your feelings about this.

Write a formal letter.

c

- Design a letterhead with your school address on it.
- Remember to include the date in your letter.
- Display newspapers which contain letters about local issues. Write letters to the newspaper, giving your views.

MAKE YOUR WORK LOOK GOOD!

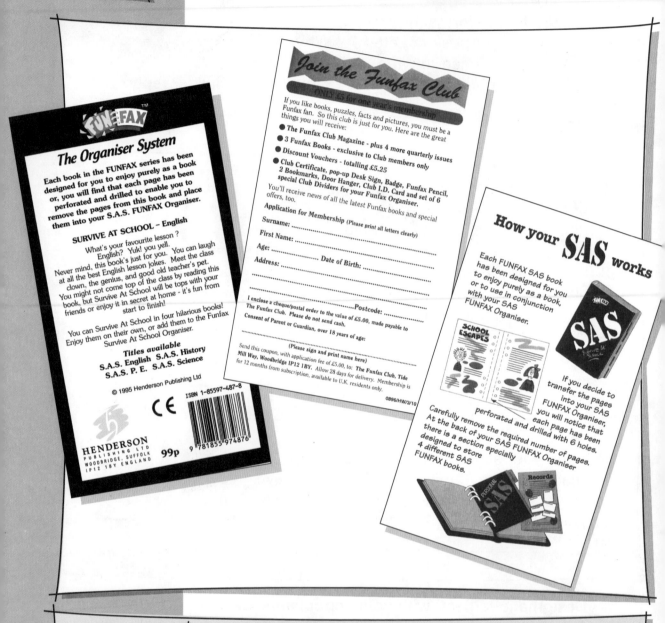

The Organiser System

Each book in the FUNFAX series has been designed for you to enjoy purely as a book or, you will find that each page has been perforated and drilled to enable you to remove the pages from this book and place them into your S.A.S. FUNFAX Organiser.

SURVIVE AT SCHOOL – English

What's your favourite lesson? English? Yuk! you yell. Never mind, this book's just for you. You can laugh at all the best English lesson jokes. Meet the class clown, the genius, and good old teacher's pet. You might not come top of the class by reading this book, but Survive At School will be tops with your friends or enjoy it in secret at home - it's fun from start to finish!

You can Survive At School in four hilarious books! Enjoy them on their own, or add them to the Funfax Survive At School Organiser.

Titles available
S.A.S. English S.A.S. History
S.A.S. P. E. S.A.S. Science

© 1995 Henderson Publishing Ltd

ISBN 1-85597-487-8

CE

HENDERSON
PUBLISHING LTD
WOODBRIDGE, SUFFOLK
IP12 1BY ENGLAND

99p

9 781855 974876

Join the Funfax Club

ONLY £5 for one year's membership

If you like books, puzzles, facts and pictures, you must be a Funfax fan. So this club is just for you. Here are the great things you will receive:

● The Funfax Club Magazine - plus 4 more quarterly issues
● 3 Funfax Books - exclusive to Club members only
● Discount Vouchers - totalling £5.25
● Club Certificate, pop-up Desk Sign, Badge, Funfax Pencil, 2 Bookmarks, Door Hanger, Club I.D. Card and set of 6 special Club Dividers for your Funfax Organiser.

You'll receive news of all the latest Funfax books and special offers, too.

Application for Membership (Please print all letters clearly)

Surname: ....

First Name: ....

Age: .... Date of Birth: ....

Address: ....

....

.... Postcode: ....

I enclose a cheque/postal order to the value of £5.00, made payable to The Funfax Club. Please do not send cash.

Consent of Parent or Guardian, over 18 years of age:

....
(Please sign and print name here)

Send this coupon, with application fee of £5.00, to: **The Funfax Club, Tide Mill Way, Woodbridge IP12 1BY.** Allow 28 days for delivery. Membership is for 12 months from subscription. available to U.K. residents only.

0896/HW/3/10

How your SAS works

Each FUNFAX SAS book has been designed for you to enjoy purely as a book, or to use in conjunction with your SAS FUNFAX Organiser.

SCHOOL ESCAPES

SAS

If you decide to transfer the pages into your SAS FUNFAX Organiser, you will notice that each page has been perforated and drilled with 6 holes.

Carefully remove the required number of pages. At the back of your SAS FUNFAX Organiser there is a section specially designed to store 4 different SAS FUNFAX books.

---

address, application, designed, exaggerate, exclusive, favourite, genius, hilarious, jingle, members, organiser, perforated, receive, required, series, slogan, special, surname, survive, transfer

a

1 Find examples of humour which make *Survive at School* (*SAS*) an attractive book.
2 The advertisement hints that you will be popular if you buy *SAS*. Do you think this is true?
3 List some of the advantages of *SAS*.
4 List the adjectives used. Do they exaggerate?

b

1 Think of five advertisements which you like. List the words they use to make things sound special.
2 Do any of them have catchy jingles or slogans? What makes them easy to remember?
3 Write a newspaper advertisement to sell your old bike. Give details and the price. Use adjectives to make it seem newer than it is, a bargain, that if you buy it you will be special, that it uses the latest technology!

c

Imagine your school has produced a magazine of pupils' work. Write different kinds of advertisements to sell your magazine in different places, for example: in a newspaper, or as a poster.

♦ Think about the size and colour in which you will write different parts of your advertisement. Make some big and bright so that they are easily spotted. Make others small and write them in black, for example: an order form.
♦ Make a display of the features advertisers use to make you want to buy something, for example: exaggerated adjectives *(New! The best!)*.

MAKE YOUR WORK LOOK GOOD!

Acknowledgements

The publishers gratefully acknowledge copyright holders for permission to use copyright material. Every effort has been made to trace copyright holders and to obtain their permission for the use of the material. The authors and publishers will gladly receive information enabling them to rectify any error or omission in subsequent editions.

Unit 1: text: from *Cider with Rosie* (Chatto & Windus, 1959), copyright © Laurie Lee 1959, reproduced by permission of PFD on behalf of the Estate of Laurie Lee; Unit 2: text: from *Carrie's War* (Penguin Puffin, 1973), copyright © Nina Bawden 1973, reproduced by permission of Curtis Brown on behalf of the author; Unit 3: text: from *The BFG* (Jonathan Cape, 1982, and Penguin Puffin, 1994), copyright © Roald Dahl 1982, reproduced by permission of David Higham Associates; Unit 4: text: from *The Wolves of Willoughby Chase* by Joan Aiken (Jonathan Cape, 1962), copyright © Joan Aiken Enterprises Ltd, reproduced by permission of A.M. Heath & Co. Ltd on behalf of the author; Unit 5: text and images: from *The Old Steam Train* (Usborne Farmyard Tales, 1999), copyright © Usborne Publishing Ltd 1999, reproduced by permission of Usborne Publishing Ltd, 83–85 Saffron Hill, London EC1M 8RT; Unit 10: text: from *Annie's Game* by Narinder Dhami (Corgi Yearling, 1999), reproduced by permission of The Random House Group Ltd; Unit 11: text: from *Buried Alive* by Jacqueline Wilson (Corgi Yearling, 1999), reproduced by permission of The Random House Group Ltd; Unit 12: text: from 'Secrets' by Anita Desai, copyright © Anita Desai 1988, first published in *Guardian Angels* edited by Stephanie Nettell (Penguin Puffin, 1988), reproduced by permission of the author c/o Rogers, Coleridge & White Ltd, 20 Powis Mews, London W11 1JN; Unit 14: text: from *Smith* by Leon Garfield (Penguin Puffin, 1968), reproduced by permission of John Johnson (Authors' Agent) Ltd; Unit 20: images: Myra Murby, reproduced by kind permission;

Unit 21: text and images: from *Incredible Wild West* by Charlotte Bingham (Dorling Kindersley, Covent Garden Books, 1995), text and illustrations copyright © Dorling Kindersley Ltd 1995, reproduced by permission of Dorling Kindersley Ltd; Unit 23: image: *Children's Games (Kinderspeile)*, 1560 by Pieter Brueghel the Elder, reproduced by permission of The Bridgeman Art Library; Unit 25: poem: adapted from 'The Poplar Field' by William Cowper; Unit 26: poem: 'High' from *The Complete Poems of Walter de la Mare* (Faber & Faber, 1969), reproduced by permission of the Literary Trustees of Walter de la Mare and the Society of Authors as their representative; Unit 28: text: from *All Abou t... The Second World War 1939–1945* by Pam Robson (*All About* series: Macdonald Young Books, 1996), reproduced by permission of Hodder & Stoughton Ltd; images: 'Women planting cabbages', copyright © Hulton Deutsch Collections/CORBIS, reproduced by permission of Corbis UK Ltd; World War II Poster 'Don't take the Squander Bug when you go shopping', reproduced by permission of the Imperial War Museum; illustration of wartime rations reproduced by permission of Peter Newark's Pictures; and illustration by John York, copyright © John York, reproduced by permission of Simon Girling Associates; Unit 30: text and images: from *Fun Fax: SAS Survive at School — English* by John McLelland, illustrated by Peter Rutherford, text and illustrations copyright © Henderson Publishing PLC/Dorling Kindersley Ltd 1995, reproduced by permission of Dorling Kindersley Ltd.

Illustrations
Francis Bacon, Unit 18
Tom Cross, Unit 22 (map and diagrams)
Linda Jeffrey, Units 1, 6, 10, 12, 14, 19, 26, 29
Carol Jonas, Units 3, 7, 8, 16 (p.35), 22 (p.46 middle), 24, 27
Paul Manning, Unit 16 (p.34)
Ruth Palmer, Units 2, 4, 11, 12, 15, 17, 25